Write It Right

with

Step by Step

by

Edna Mae Burnam

To my grandson, David Bender

ISBN 978-1-4234-3601-0

WILLIS MUSIC

EXCLUSIVELY DISTRIBUTED BY

HAL•LEONARD®
CORPORATION
7777 W. BLUEMOUND RD. P.O. BOX 13819 MILWAUKEE, WI 53213

Visit Hal Leonard Online at
www.halleonard.com

TO THE TEACHER

The written work in this book is designed to correlate exactly with Edna Mae Burnam's STEP BY STEP—Book Three.

At the beginning of each lesson, at the top of the page, is a notation giving the exact page in the correlated STEP BY STEP book at which the respective WRITE IT RIGHT lessons may be introduced. (Each lesson is planned on the musical steps which have been introduced up to and including this page.)

The WRITE IT RIGHT lessons will both train the student to be accurate and afford the teacher a means of checking the student's comprehension of the musical steps which he or she is learning.

A special effort has been made to incorporate variety in the written work and to choose subject matter which is appealing to the student.

I sincerely hope that the WRITE IT RIGHT lessons will be an enjoyable experience.

Edna Mae Burnam

When the student reaches page 9 of Edna Mae Burnam's STEP BY STEP—Book Three, he is ready to do Lesson One.

3

LESSON ONE

HATS

Here are some hats to decorate.
See how the treble clefs decorate hat number one?

Put some **bass clefs**
in hat two.

Put some **hold signs**
in hat three.

Put some **accent signs**
in hat four.

Put some **staccato marks**
in hat five.

Put some **sharp signs**
in hat six.

Put some **flat signs**
in hat seven.

Put some **natural signs**
in hat eight.

Put some **eighth rests**
in hat nine.

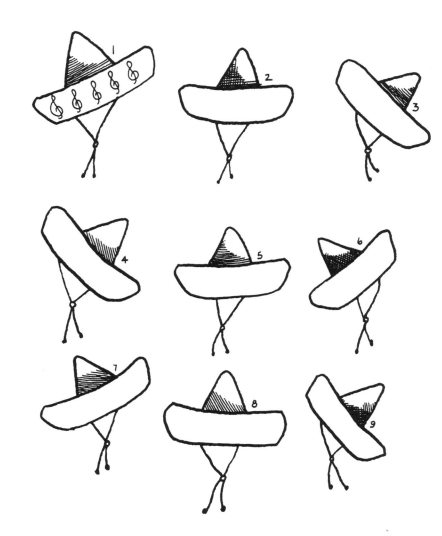

Write the right **note** or **rest** needed in each box to complete the following measures.

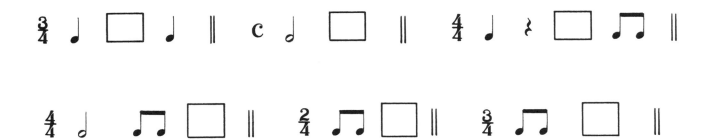

PIGEONS

These pigeons are trained to fly home.

Draw a line from each pigeon to its right place in the keyboard pigeon house.

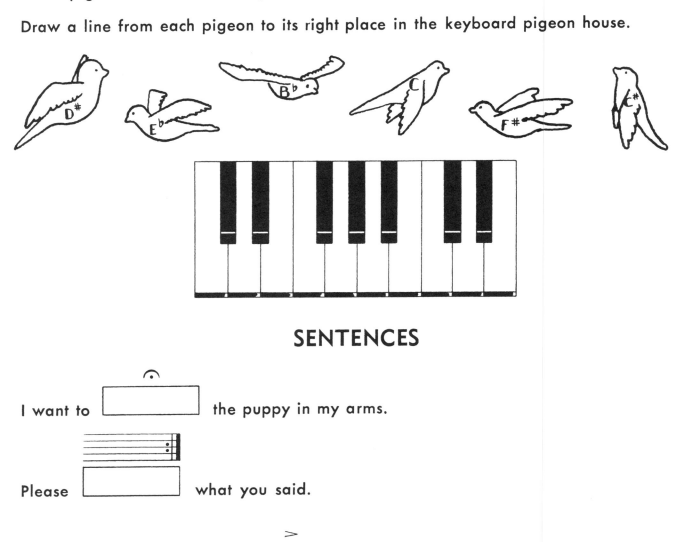

SENTENCES

I want to ⌒ ⬜ the puppy in my arms.

Please ⬜ what you said.

When we play a waltz, we ⬜ the note count of every measure.

QUESTIONS

When you see this time signature, how many counts are there in each measure? _____

What does this mean? _____

What is this sign called? _____

What is this mark called? _____

What is the name of this sign? _____

LESSON TWO
GOLDFISH

Write the right letter names of the goldfish notes in the boxes.

If you get all of them right, you may have a goldfish.

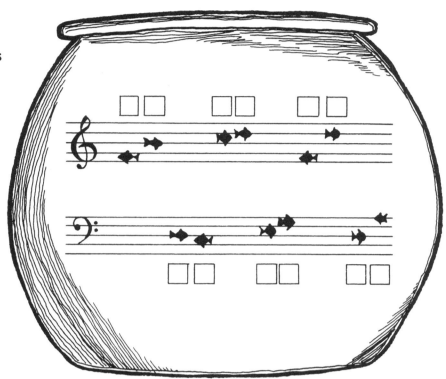

MATCH UPS

Draw a line to connect the musical signs in column **Two** with the word or words which explain them in column **One.**

One	Two
soft	
very soft	⌢
moderately soft	>
loud	.
moderately loud	*ff*
very loud	*pp*
accent	*mf*
staccato	*mp*
hold	*p*
first and second ending	*f*

METRONOMES

Fill in the measures below each metronome with the right number of notes or rests as called for by the time signatures.

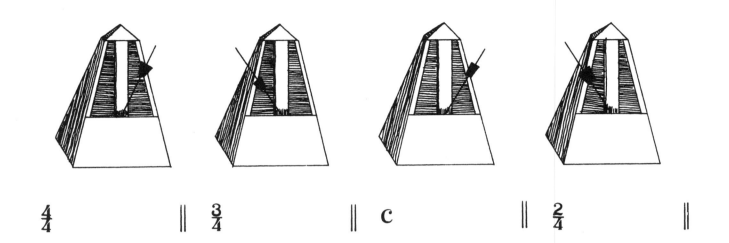

A SENTENCE

Write the right letter names of the notes not named.
Read the sentence aloud.

_ I _ M O N _ S _ R _ _ _ _ _ U T I _ U L.

QUESTIONS

When you come to a first and second ending and you are playing the piece for the first time, do you play the first ending and also the second ending?   _____

When you are playing the same piece for the second time, do you skip the first ending and just play the second ending?   _____

Does **forte** mean to play loud?   _____

Does **pianissimo** mean to play very soft?   _____

LESSON THREE

LOLLIPOP

Write the right letter names of the notes in the boxes.

If you get all of them right, you may have a lollipop.

BLOCKS

Put a **sharp** in No. 1.

Put a **flat** in No. 2.

Put a **natural** in No. 3.

Put an **accent** in No. 4.

Put a **staccato** in No. 5.

Put a **hold** in No. 6.

Put a **treble clef** in No. 7.

Put a **bass clef** in No. 8.

Put a **quarter note** in No. 9.

Put an **eighth note** in No. 10.

Put an **eighth rest** in No. 11.

Put a **quarter rest** in No. 12.

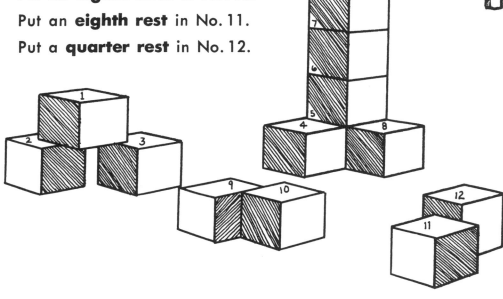

BELLS

Here are some ringing bells.

Some ring louder than others.

Draw an arrow from each bell to the word or words which tell how loud that bell is ringing.

very soft

very loud

soft

loud

moderately loud

moderately soft

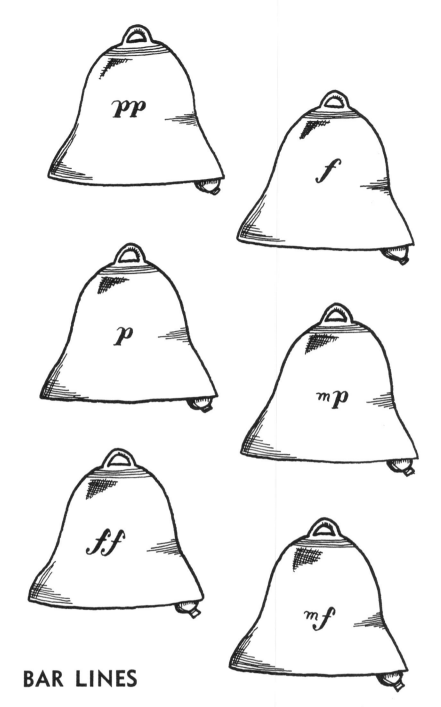

BAR LINES

Draw bar lines in the right places, and put a double bar at the end of this line of notes.

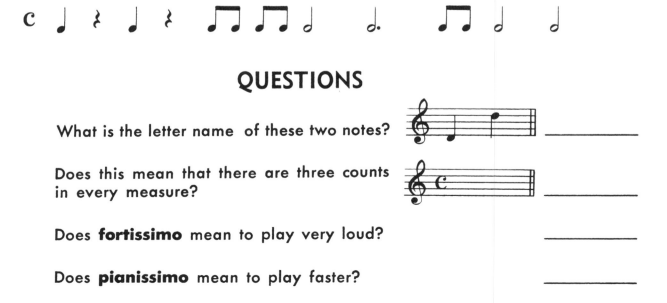

QUESTIONS

What is the letter name of these two notes? _____

Does this mean that there are three counts in every measure? _____

Does **fortissimo** mean to play very loud? _____

Does **pianissimo** mean to play faster? _____

LESSON FOUR
LANTERNS

Write the right letter names of the notes in the boxes.

If you get all of them right, you may have a lantern.

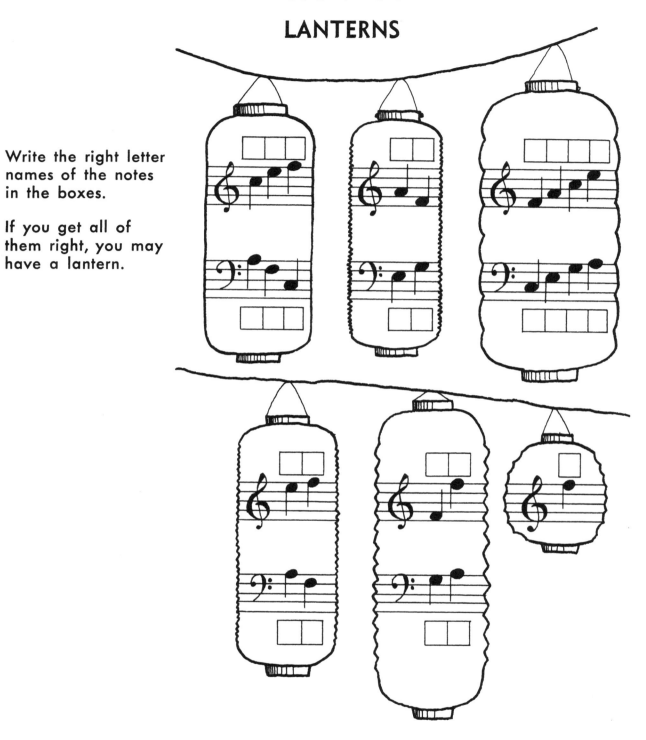

Write the right words needed in the long boxes.

This means to play gradually

This means to play gradually

ritard means to play gradually

FOOTBALLS

By adding up the notes and rests contained in each football, you may find out the exact number of touchdowns that they scored in the last game.

Write the right answers in the boxes.

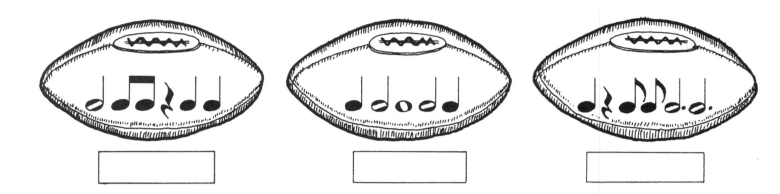

NUMBER THE LINES

Write the right number of each line in the boxes.

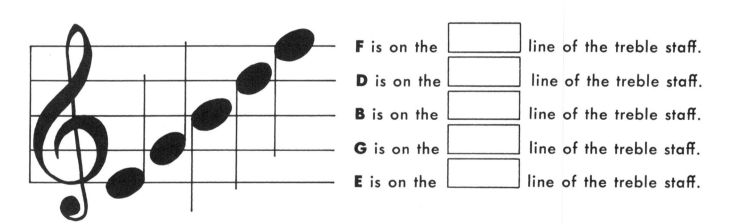

F is on the [ ] line of the treble staff.

D is on the [ ] line of the treble staff.

B is on the [ ] line of the treble staff.

G is on the [ ] line of the treble staff.

E is on the [ ] line of the treble staff.

QUESTIONS

What is the letter name of this note? _____

Do **ritard** and **rit.** have the same meaning? _____

Does **ritard** mean to play faster? _____

Does this sign ——— mean to accent? _____

Does this sign ——— mean gradually slower? _____

LESSON FIVE

A BLIMP

Write the right letter names of the notes in the boxes.

If you get all of them right, you may have a ride in the blimp.

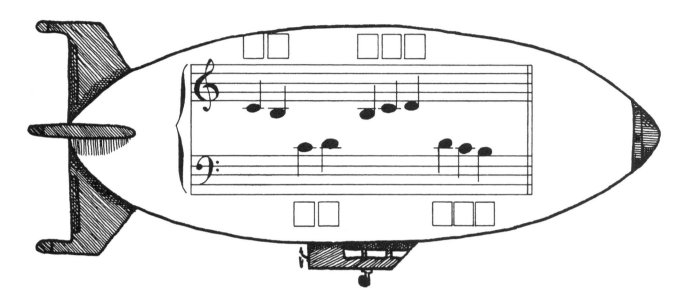

JUMP OVERS

Which hand jumps over the other hand in this line of music?

Play the music.

Which hand jumps over the other hand in this line of music?

Play the music.

COUNTS

Write the right counting under each line of notes.

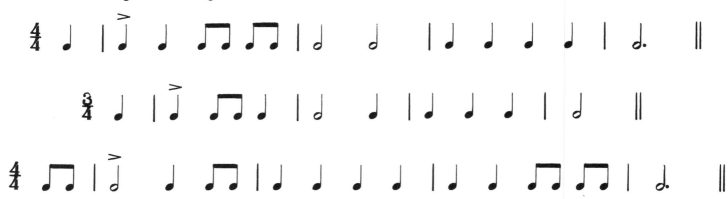

SENTENCES

Write the right words in the boxes to complete the sentences.
Read each line aloud.

Ice cream is [*p*] and [*legato*].

A whisper is [*pp*].

A police car siren is [*ff*].

I will sit down and [ɣ] for a while.

I will [⌢] the last note in this [ ].

QUESTIONS

Do these two notes have
the same letter name?   _____

Do these two notes have
the same letter name?   _____

When the student reaches page 35 of Edna Mae Burnam's STEP BY STEP—Book Three, he is ready to do Lesson Six.

LESSON SIX

CHINESE CHIMES

Decorate the chimes.

Put some **sharp signs** in this chime.

Put some **flat signs** in this chime.

Put a **hold sign** in this chime.

Put an **eighth rest** in this chime.

Put some **staccato marks** in this chime.

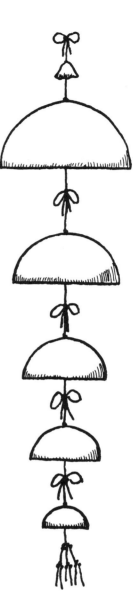

A HAMMOCK

Write the right letter names of the notes in the boxes.
If you get all of them right, you may swing in the hammock.

COFFEE POTS

The notes and rests tell how many cups of coffee each coffee pot will make.

Add up the counts contained in each pot, and write the right answers in the boxes.

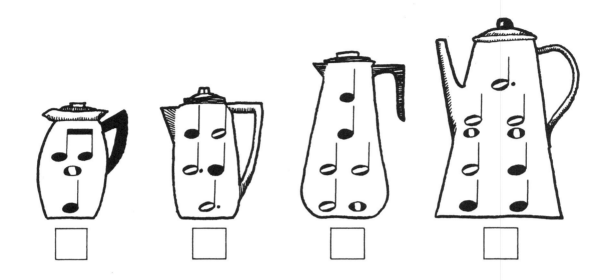

BAR LINES

Draw bar lines in the right places, and put a double bar at the end.

QUESTIONS

What do turkeys say?

_ O _ L _, _ O _ L _.

What do birdies say?

T W _ _ T, T W _ _ T.

When the student reaches page 39 of Edna Mae Burnam's STEP BY STEP—Book Three, he is ready to do Lesson Seven.

15

LESSON SEVEN

A LONG BALLOON

Write the right letter name
of the notes in the boxes.

If you get one
wrong, the balloon
will "POP".

Be careful!

VEGETABLES

Build a **major triad** on the note in each vegetable.

Write the right notes for the triad, and put the **stem** on the chord.

Put the letter name of each triad you build in the box below.

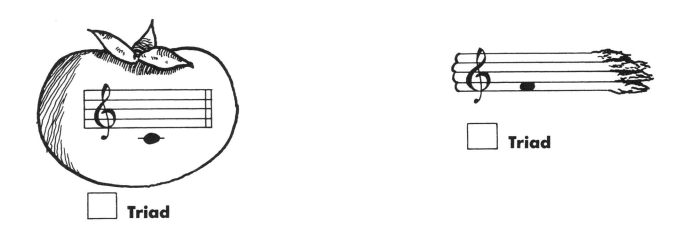

☐ **Triad**

☐ **Triad**

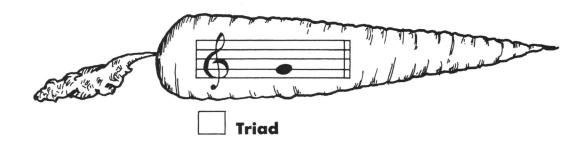

☐ **Triad**

ICE CREAM CONE

How many bites will it take
to eat this ice cream cone?

Add up the counts of all of
the notes, and write the right
answer in the box.

If you get the right answer,
you may have an ice cream cone!

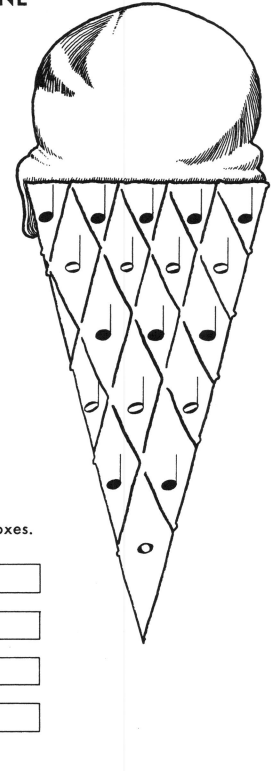

MEANINGS

Write the right meanings in the boxes.

mf means to play

mp means to play

ff means to play

pp means to play

QUESTIONS

How many notes make a **triad?**

_____

How many sharps are there in
the key of **G major?**

_____

How many flats are there in
the key of **F major?**

_____

When the student reaches page 44 of Edna Mae Burnam's STEP BY STEP—Book Three, he is ready to do Lesson Eight.

LESSON EIGHT

SUITCASES

Here are some locked suitcases. Find the right key for each suitcase.

Draw a line from each key to the suitcase it will unlock.

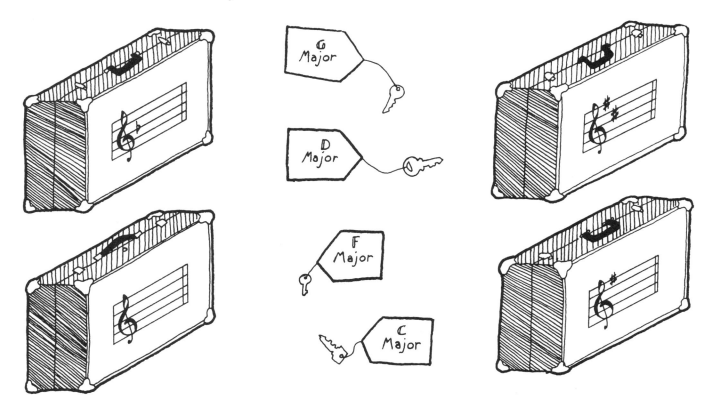

RAINBOW

Write in the right names of the notes, and find out something about a rainbow.

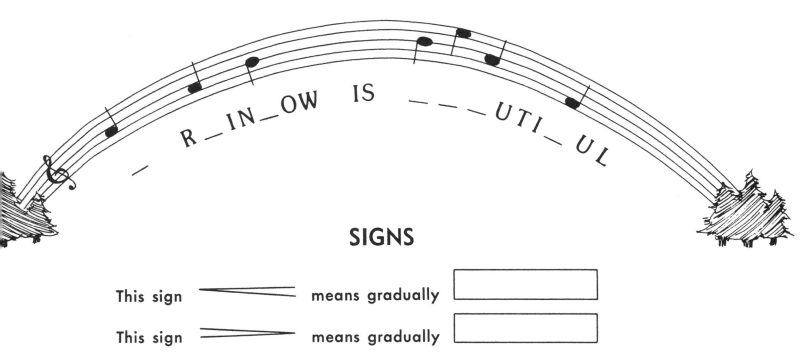

_ R _ IN _ OW IS _ _ _ _ UTI _ UL

SIGNS

This sign ⟍ means gradually [   ]

This sign ⟋ means gradually [   ]

SKI LIFT

Add up all of the counts of the notes and rests in order to see how many minutes it takes to ride to the top of the ski lift.

Put the answer in the box at the top.

QUESTIONS

Does a piece of music **always** begin on count "one"? _____

Does a piece of music **always** have the same key signature to the end? _____

LESSON NINE

A MESSAGE

Write the right names of the notes.

Read the message aloud.

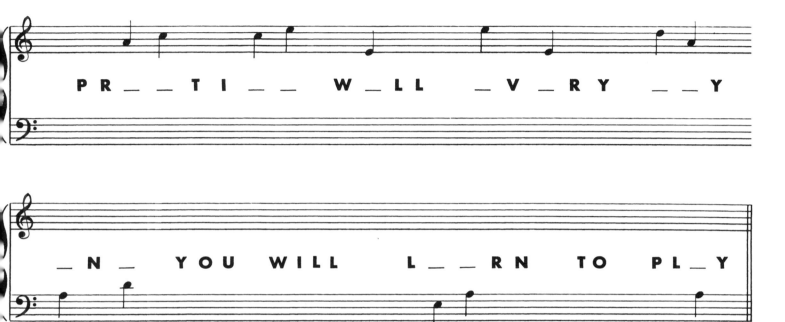

PR _ _ T I _ _   W _ L L   _ V _ R Y   _ _ Y

_ N _   Y O U   W I L L   L _ _ R N   T O   P L _ Y

HATS

Build a **major triad** on the note in each hat.

Write the right notes for the triad and put on the **stem.**

Put the **letter name** of each triad in the box below.

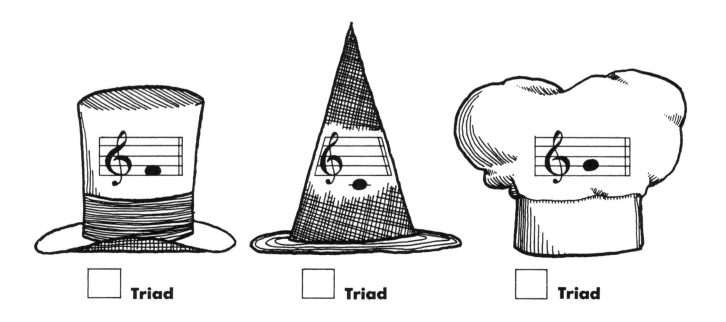

☐ **Triad**   ☐ **Triad**   ☐ **Triad**

INCENSE

Add up all of the counts of the notes and rests in order to see how many hours the fragrance from the incense will last.

Put the number of hours in the box.

 hours

MACRAME

Decorate this macrame.

Put a **sharp** in every circle.

Put a **flat** in every diamond.

Put a **natural** in every heart.

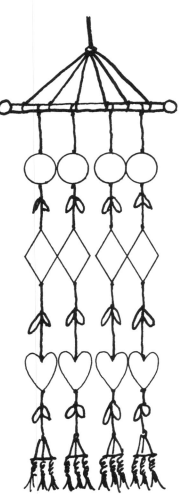

QUESTIONS

What key signature has one flat?

What is the flat?

What key signature has two sharps?

What are the two sharps?

What key signature has no sharps or flats?

Major

Major

Major

Lesson Ten is a review correlated with all of Edna Mae Burnam's STEP BY STEP—Book Three.

21

LESSON TEN

NOTES

Write the right letter name of the notes in the boxes.

Draw a line from each box to the right key on the keyboard.

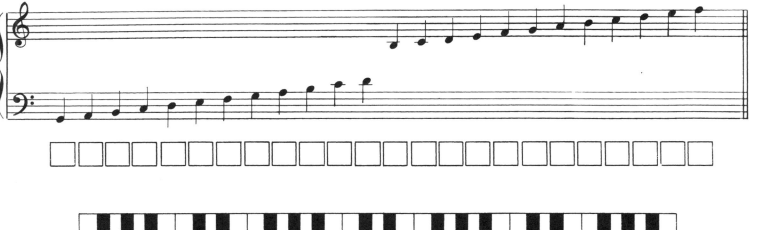

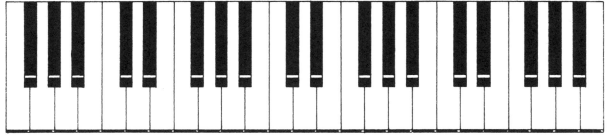

KEY SIGNATURES

Write the right name of the key signatures in the boxes.

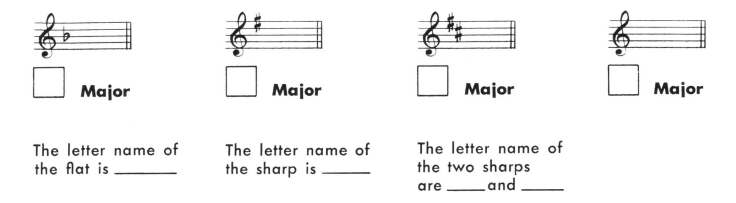

The letter name of the flat is _____

The letter name of the sharp is _____

The letter name of the two sharps are _____ and _____

NOTE AND REST VALUES

Add up all of the note and rest counts, and put the total in the box at the end.

WHIZ QUIZ
ARROWS

Draw an arrow from each abbreviation in column one to the words telling the meaning in column two.

mf	very loud
p	very soft
pp	medium loud
f	soft
mp	loud
l. h.	left hand
ff	medium soft

Draw an arrow from each musical direction on the left to the matching sign on the right.

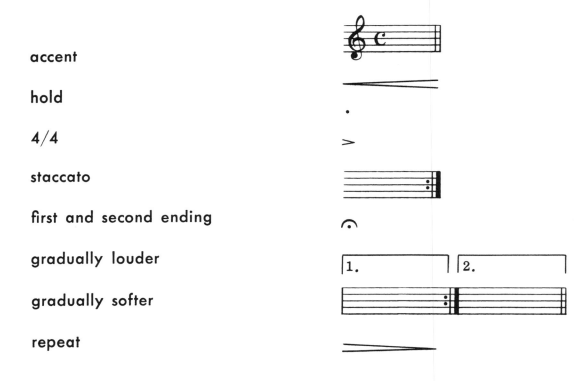

accent

hold

4/4

staccato

first and second ending

gradually louder

gradually softer

repeat

QUESTIONS

How many notes are there in a triad? _____

In 4/4 time, a pick up note is usually
on what count? _____

In 3/4 time, a pick up note is usually
on what count? _____

Certificate of Merit

This is to certify that

_____

has successfully completed

BOOK THREE
OF
EDNA MAE BURNAM'S

WRITE IT RIGHT

and is now eligible for promotion to

BOOK FOUR

_____ Teacher

Date _____

Edna Mae Burnam

Edna Mae Burnam (1907–2007) is one of the most respected names in piano pedagogy. She began her study of the instrument at age seven with lessons from her mother, and went on to major in piano at the University of Washington and Chico State Teacher's College in Los Angeles. In 1935, she sold "The Clock That Stopped"—one of her original compositions still in print today—to a publisher for $20. In 1937, Burnam began her long and productive association with Florence, Kentucky-based Willis Music, who signed her to her first royalty contract. In 1950, she sent manuscripts to Willis for an innovative piano series comprised of short and concise warm-up exercises—she drew stick figures indicating where the "real" illustrations should be dropped in. That manuscript, along with the original stick figures, became the best-selling *A Dozen a Day* series, which has sold more than 25 million copies worldwide; the stick-figure drawings are now icons.

Burnam followed up on the success of *A Dozen a Day* with her *Step by Step Piano Course*. This method teaches students the rudiments of music in a logical order and manageable pace, for gradual and steady progress. She also composed hundreds of individual songs and pieces, many based on whimsical subjects or her international travels. These simple, yet effective learning tools for children studying piano have retained all their charm and unique qualities, and remain in print today in the Willis catalog. Visit **www.halleonard.com** to browse all available piano music by Edna Mae Burnam.